THE MOST POWERFUL PERSON ON EARTH !

PATRICIA OGILVIE

Copyright © 2022 by Patricia Ogilvie
Revised 2nd Edition

All rights reserved.

Published by Prorisk Enterprises Ltd.
Box 253, Alberta Beach, Alberta,
Canada T0E 0A0
ISBN: 10:0978052013
ISBN-13: 978-0978052010 (ProRisk Ent Ltd)

The content in this book is for general educational purposes only and should not be construed as medical advice or instruction. The information should not serve as a substitute for professional medical care.

No part of this book may be reproduced in any form or by any electronic or mechanical means, including information storage and retrieval systems, without written permission from the author, except for the use of brief quotations in a book review.

CONTENTS

Acknowledgments	vii
Introduction	ix
1. Day 1: The Learning Mindset	1
2. Day 2: 90/10 Rule	4
3. Day 3: Repitition & Visualization	7
4. Day 4: Attitude Adjustments	10
5. Day 5: Transform Worry into Happy	13
6. Day 6: Change Happens	16
7. Day 7: A Week of Creativity	20
8. Day 8: Validation	24
9. Day 9: Relationship Factor	27
10. Day 10: Life is Your Mirror	31
11. Day 11: Tap into Your Power	35
12. Day 12: Vision Mastery	38
13. Day 13: Time Mastery	45
14. Day 14: Memory & Belief Mastery	49
15. Day 15: Forgiveness Mastery	54
16. Day 16: Worthiness Mastery	57
17. Day 17: Managing Stress	63
18. Day 18: Interpretations	66
19. Day 19: Havingness Mastery	69
20. Day 20: Receiving Mastery	71
21. Day 21: Mastering Peacefulness	73
22. Creating Space in a Crowd	76
23. Transform to Self-Esteem	78
Bibliography	81
About the Author	83

This booklet is dedicated to my parents, Anne and Paul who remind me through my memories how intuitively I have always known my own power ... especially when I least understood mirrored influences.

It's also written for my life buddies, David, Terry and Sonia. I love you so much!

And Randy, my husband who has come along for a ride of his life—shifting and changing and moving and growing. I can't think of anyone else who would have joined me in this energetic journey of experimenting from the inside out.

Thank you, and I love you all.

ACKNOWLEDGMENTS

 There will soon be no more priests. Their work is done... Every man shall be his own priest.

— WALT WHITMAN

Good tools, winning ideas and simple strategies which focus your attention on success, also have the power to start a fire in your belly.

So congratulations for attracting this special little book. You are on a journey of discovery that will entice you, rejoice you and flavor your life. Let the flames begin!

Let me ask you this. Where does that fire in your belly motivation come from? Mine hit me back in 1990 when I began writing poetry. I was inspired by Mary Oliver's "The Journey." It begins like this:

> One day you finally knew
> what you had to do, and began,
> though the voices around you
> kept shouting
> their bad advice ...

Her message shakes me to the core each time I read

these words. It shakes me hard and demands I look inside myself at how honest I am living my life.

In an interview for the Bloomsbury Review, Mary said, "I feel that the function of the poet is to be somehow instructive and opinionated, useful even if only as a devil's advocate."

You're right Mary. The questions we must all ask ourselves are, "Am I telling myself the truth? And if so, how does it feel?"

Well, Mary Oliver, thank you for reminding me to look squarely into my own eyes each time I look into that mirror and say to myself, *Patricia, how does it feel to me?*

I didn't want those other voices telling me what I could or couldn't feel, do, or want! It was time for me to hear my own voice. How about you?

INTRODUCTION

The Only Life You Can Serve

Once upon a time ...

Well, fairy tales start this way. And this is not a fairy tale storybook. My story is real, and I bet you could relate in many ways. So let's get started on a journey of discovery, awareness, change and fun!

I'm just going to get right to the point. Here's the story that influenced my self-worth.

One of the most vivid memories of my childhood was the experience of my first job, babysitting.

By the time I turned twelve years old, I had several years of experience helping my mom babysit my younger siblings. There were four of us in five years, and I was the oldest. But I don't hold that against anyone. Nope, not me.

The truth is, I enjoyed being the oldest for the most part. It meant more responsibility, and I actually enjoyed that.

Growing up with younger siblings, I was asked to

share my toys, like my favorite cardboard school bus box that held crayons, books, pens, and all sorts of exciting colored papers and trinkets. No problem. My sister chewed it up nicely, so all the wonderful content was eventually relegated to a paper grocery bag.

I was asked to help mom clean the house and tidy up the messes the boys brought in like dirt, dust, twigs and straw.

It seemed as if the sweeping and wiping was just done. When I looked into the room I just finished dusting and organizing, there it was, upside down and messy again! But, no problem.

Then one day, I was asked to babysit two little boys of close friends of my parents. No problem!

It was a New Year's Eve dance and my parents left me to babysit for their friends who went along to the dance with them. I enjoyed the experience, played with the boys, and they went to sleep after a snack, a song, a story, and a hug.

I didn't fall asleep. I made sure I was awake just in case. That was my job to make sure that the boys were safe and everything was alright.

Shortly after one a.m. the adults arrived. The lady was pleased and handed me money. Wow, I thought. This was way more than I expected and I was happy my first real job was so lucrative!

Then it happened. Dad intervened. He took the bills out of my hand, gave them back to the lady and said, "Hey, for friends, it's free."

The lady didn't argue. I was dumbfounded and said

nothing. I went home feeling sad, confused, and empty-handed.

Since I was young, I didn't dare question what just happened. But after that, I kept refusing babysitting opportunities. It wasn't until my last year of high school I decided I wanted to earn some money besides an allowance that was given only when necessary. I asked my parents if I could get a "real" job as a cashier at the local pharmacy.

They said yes. But mom or dad had to drive me the twelve kilometres into town for my shifts. Then they had to pick me up. I had a driver's license by then; however, we didn't have an extra vehicle. I felt as if I was a burden. But I ignored the feelings.

That job motivated me to go to university and become a pharmacist. I don't think my parents realized at the time how influenced I had become to further education and a career. I think they were surprised.

You see, growing up in a rural community with old-world beliefs, I believe that my dad was terrified to have me educated. I could sense that he thought it was a waste of time and money. He believed that being female meant only one thing. I would get married and have kids. And then what? He would be right. A waste of time and a good chunk of change he didn't really have to send me for higher education was wasted.

I still didn't say anything.

My mom convinced him to give me a chance. She was somewhat ahead of her time in that respect, always supporting us girls to do even more with our lives than she did which was to get married and raise a family. She

INTRODUCTION

found out about a Northern Alberta Bursary program that would finance my education if I in turn, worked back my loan in Northern Alberta. I was cool with that.

So I went to university and still felt sick with guilt and fear about "stealing" my dad's money even though most of the tuition was paid through the bursary. I became very sick with stomach cramps. At times, the tension was so extreme; I would ride an ambulance to a nearby hospital just in case it turned out to be something else like appendicitis or rupture. It was always the fear. I learned much later in life it was stuck energy that needed to be recognized and released. But more on that later.

That fear, on numerous occasions, convinced me to quit. But each time, my mother, bless her heart, intervened and talked me out of it. She knew it was fear and why didn't I just finish off the term, write my exams and decide after that? So I did, and I passed the term. And each term went the same.

Four years later, I graduated with my degree, and instead of pharmacy and considering starting my own business, I became a junior high school teacher. This surprised me.

But what surprised me more was that my dad was proud that I had something to back me up if I ever had to take care of myself.

What? Now he was glad? In all honesty, I felt a tad of resentment that after all, he was proud of me. I can't explain, but teaching was not my first priority and because he was glad I was teaching, I think I unconsciously quit after one year because of more erroneous thinking. I begin an inner turmoil of playing a victim and

INTRODUCTION

I admit that I used him as my excuse to sabotage a lot of things in my life.

Now, please don't get me wrong here. I was grateful— oh so grateful for having the opportunity in the end. It was all those stomach aches, fear, anger and ongoing sabotaging that kept me awake at nights. It was this inner turmoil that needed attention.

This book and these next twenty-one days became the process I used to finally bust out of the sabotaging energetic hold I allowed for years. I finally took my power back and healed my stomach pains. Then I began a successful coaching practice.

I not only became fascinated with the constructs of human potential, but I also incorporated energy transformation concepts into my training in logical environments like finance and business.

Originally, I thought my interest in energy and belief transformation was just a personal interest of mine. But what I realized was that psychology and the concepts of beliefs was the key to success in personal and professional arenas. Actually, spiritual and energetic concepts are critical in every walk of life where relationships and communication play a part.

I'm sure you'll agree that everything is about relationships and communication! I'm hoping that by the end of this book you will also agree that everything is energy!

The more I worked with clients struggling to put their finances in order or put a financial and business plan together, or simply try to determine what their next step would be, the clearer it became to me that energy and belief systems had everything to do with building successful business, increasing confidence and more money.

While it's important to have a good income and future plans and strategies in place, I've never met anyone who was able to apply basic strategies for building a business or personal relationship without hitting a ceiling, failing or quitting before they reached a level of success. That is unless they had their emotional and psychological life in order.

I can say with absolute certainty that for me, contrary to what people think, the biggest barriers to personal and professional success aren't ineffective training or wrong ideas about business or love.

I realized that the biggest barrier to succeeding in business, in my personal relationships *and* making money was related to the way I was thinking and feeling about myself. That's how I managed my life.

> *My success and happiness was directly related to my initial experiences as a child about money, about work, and about relationship success in general.*

I began to see a pattern in my personal life. I'd get excited about a beau, a year later things would grow tense, sour and the relationship ended. I saw the same pattern in my professional life. I'd get excited about putting a plan of action together, formulate some terrific ideas, spend money on a blog or website, and then things would taper off.

INTRODUCTION

Then I'd hear a voice inside my head that asks, "Why did you quit?" Rarely did I have a viable answer.

Instead I'd hear a lot of "I don't know. It's too hard. I can't seem to make any money at this. I don't belong in this niche. He wasn't right for me!" And so on.

What I uncovered was that somewhere along the way, a deeply rooted emotional issue was the culprit that made my life a roller coaster of good and bad experiences.

The underlying issues I'm talking about can take on many disguises. For example, you might be in a stressful relationship. It's difficult enough to make life changes for yourself as it is. But without the support of a spouse or family, the drama intensifies and it seems easier to just give up than build a dream.

Maybe your efforts to cope with the stress of financial troubles, overwork if you don't have help, or working with difficult people if you do have help, are sucking the joy out of you. You're left with little to no energy, you don't feel good, so you rethink your efforts.

If you're like me, you might be carrying emotional scars from disheartening experiences when you were younger. Maybe your authority figures like parents, teachers or other care givers, wounded your self-esteem and self image. So you decided that you weren't capable of earning money or serving others where each of you wins.

Maybe they laughed at your ideas and invalidated your dreams. This could easily cause doubt, conflict, and inner turmoil that pop up exactly on queue when you're ready to move forward.

INTRODUCTION

If any of this resonates for you, then know that there's an obstacle in your path. Likewise, these early experiences, if not adequately addressed as energy to be released and transformed, could surface over and over as habits you may not even be aware of.

Your own self-talk could be superimposing your communications to increasing a client base. Your mind chatter, if not aware, could be deliberately sabotaging your love life. And you don't know why.

For example, if you are having trouble staying motivated in your work, and you find yourself sabotaging your time, and use excuses like "it's them" or "chalking it up to PMS!", there is only one place to go.

It's deeper and different than the surface stuff. In fact, the outer environment is giving you clues where to look inside yourself.

You have to be willing to look a little deeper. There's another layer. It could be as simple as a belief that "No one's gonna want it anyway." or "I don't like myself." or "I'm not good enough." or "I'm insignificant and not worthy of your love." or my favorite, "There must be something wrong with me."

The truth is you always know what it is. Now it's time to get the excuses out in the open and let them go.

But that requires taking a good look at yourself and your motivations, your fears, and your self-talk. All you have to do is be willing and ask yourself for clarification.

You've got to explore and acknowledge your thoughts and feelings, including those that you may have been disregarding for quite a while.

Your goal could be to change what's going on inside

INTRODUCTION

you. When that happens, changing your routines, your focus, and honestly addressing failures will naturally shift into successes.

The emotional and psychological side of business success and relationship communication has always been important to me. I decided to further my understanding and chose to add several philosophical and energy transformation programs to my credibility. So now, certified as a coach trained in intuitive skills to help people transform distorted thinking into supportive visions, my clients actually enjoy the process and go deeper to find issues and blocks preventing success.

When people recognize that beliefs get in the way of success, most people release the energy behind the beliefs and take back their power. They begin to take new actions to support feeling better about their life journeys.

I alluded earlier to several things that can stand in the way of increasing financial and emotional success in business.

These include bad relationships, stressful work environments, unsupportive family and spouses and deeper emotional scars like the time my dad took hard-earned babysitting money out of my hands.

I can tell you that the babysitting incident stayed with me for a long time and I realized I thought of myself as an undeserving person. Actually what I decided about myself back then was that it was my fault I didn't get paid. I didn't know what I did or didn't do, but it was my fault. A kid's brain isn't always logical. The real reason was deeper. The real reason was I wasn't good enough, obviously, and they found out!

You could have experienced something similar.

There are ways to short circuit some of the digging. But what can't be short circuited is your willingness to find out what the issues really are.

I don't exaggerate when I say that success undergoes transformations. The largest transition is from childhood to adulthood, from a single person to living with another, from dependent student to independent income generator, from an employee to self-employed. The changes are obvious on the outside. But are you changing inside? Are you letting go of child hurts going into adult situations? That's the thing—not everyone leaves behind child patterns. And why not? They just don't know how.

Life is full of transformation and life's ease is about how to smoothly transition into each. Yes, how you handle them and how you accept and let go of the past makes the transformation difficult or smooth.

Everyone's journey will be different. So let's find out more about how to begin your journey into self-discovery.

HOW THIS BOOK WORKS

This book is really about how to improve your emotional well-being. This is the book that's going to help you get to the bottom of why you keep sabotaging your success and what makes you stop trying.

If you've never gotten started in the first place, this is the book that's going to help you understand why. Everything in these pages is designed to help you attend to what's going on inside you (your mind and your way of thinking). Then you can go about your real business. You can get on with the business of improving your income level, increase your client base, build your project scopes and rebuild your self-confidence even greater than it is now.

So what's the process?

One or more of these tips and strategies may strike a chord with you. Whichever it is, going through this simple process will get the wheels turning in your head and transform energy in your heart. Once you do the recommended activity, write what you experience each day. This is your private book. Write in it. Use it to its full potential. Carry it wherever you go, and write in it whenever you can. Take the time to notice your feelings and thoughts. And have fun.

There's only one life you can serve and that is your own. You are the most powerful person on earth when it comes to making your life journey filled with value and love. And I know you know this.

So thanks for hanging in there so far.

Great job today!

Chapter One
DAY 1: THE LEARNING MINDSET

Do you consider yourself open-minded? Are you on board with the current state in the evolution of mass consciousness you know, that spiritual pocket from which we are born, shapes your current life and into which you will pass back into? And that everything is energy?

If I've lost you already, be patient, it gets easier and more interesting each day. If you have a learning mindset and see yourself as open, successful and willing to learn regardless of the obstacles, then keep on reading. If you want a new experience, keep on reading.

> *"What the mind of man can conceive and believe, it can achieve."*
>
> — NAPOLEAN HILL, THINK AND GROW RICH.

Hill makes a good point. Even as your mind leads you

in a direction, you also feel things about your goals and dreams. I'm referring to the energy your brain emits. What you *feel* is the glue that attracts more of the same to you. As humans, we are energetic beings. Energy vibrates inside and outside of our bodies. That's how we create our lives. We vibrate our experiences into our immediate environments. We are charged and electrical.

Have you ever experienced the electric ball at the science fair? You touch the ball as it produces electrical currents and it makes your hair stand on end. Or rub a balloon on your hair and see how it sticks to a wall? That's an electrical charge. And that's the energy we're talking about here.

Your thoughts are just like that electrical charge. And if you are rubbed the wrong way, you stick to a wall of limitation and grief. I think you know what I'm saying here.

So day one of your journey is to challenge yourself right now to re-program your thinking. I want you to understand and acknowledge that you are energy. You are a mass of vibrating bits and pieces of cells and atoms.

Day one is to challenge yourself right now to re-program how you see your current situation. Your hesitations, fears, anger, confusion and frustrations are built on blocks from your past. How you feel about your past can and does influence you today unless you decide in this moment to change how you see yourself.

Here's an example. I used to feel bitter about my babysitting experience. I couldn't let it go for a very long time. So over the years, in various work situations, I had that deep sense in the pit of my stomach that I might not get paid if I screw up. I quit every job about the time that the old belief took on momentum and I convinced myself "they" will find something wrong with me. "They'll" figure out that if things get broke, it's my fault. I didn't understand any better at the time. If someone looked at me sideways, I was spooked.

So your challenge today is to refuse to let old stories ruin your current experience. You'll become far more effective with this small shift in thinking.

Let them go.

ACTION STEP

Ask yourself," How much resistance are you in, this very moment, to learning more about yourself?" Place your hand on your heart, and ask, "How much are you vested in staying the same because you want to be right about how life works in your world?" What does your heart say?

If your resistance justifies staying stuck, you might want to ask yourself, "How much of you is pushing or fighting against changing to get more peace of mind?"

Now imagine a gauge with a dial in front of you. Ask that gauge how much resistance you have to any or all of the things in your life that stress you?

Reach out and turn the dial down a bit. You will feel better even if it's just a small notch. That's it; dial it down until you can feel yourself freeing resistance to learn more. Allow yourself to make your life journey effortless.

Now you're using the most powerful tool to get what you want—your imagination! Remember to use this tool whenever you feel resistant about anything.

Chapter Two

DAY 2: 90/10 RULE

"Whew ..." I hear you saying. "What's in store today? What's this book really about anyway?"

You may not believe me when I say that the stories you tell yourself every single day have lead up to this moment!

And those stories are either made up by yourself or someone else who told you things about you.

Here's the good news.

More than 90% of the beliefs you operate out of and live by are someone else's. Less than 10% are your own.

Here's what I mean. A friend of mine who has been a follower of personal growth techniques for almost twenty years said this the other day.

She discovered a bunch of negative beliefs she had about completing a project that had a due date looming. So we went through some of those beliefs.

"What if ..."

"I hope I don't ..."
"I should have said ..."
"The client won't like me if ..."
"I always have a problem with ..."
"I probably won't be able to finish anyway ..."
"I can't believe how stupid I was to try this ..."

She then said, "I've been working on these beliefs for over twenty years. But something is still there. It's like the beliefs are sticky fly paper strips that won't move!

So why don't those beliefs move out? The reason for the difficulty and longevity was that those were not hers in the first place!

You can't budge, shift or change what's not yours.

You can only let them go and send them back to their original owners... parents, siblings, friends, bosses, or whoever told you something about yourself that has plagued you most of your life!

ACTION STEP

Find a comfortable chair in a quiet place. Sit upright with hands in your lap and feet on the floor. Close your eyes, take a deep breath and as you exhale, imagine your whole body relaxing. And again, take a deep breath and relax.

Keep your eyes closed and imagine that you know where the tension or blocked energy sits in your body. Notice that it's stuck there. Breathe deeply again and imagine you are expanding your body to allow it to have more space.

Pretend you are expanding space in your imagination until your body is as big as the room you sit in. Give that energy block as much space as it wants.

Good job! Now imagine that there is an energetic grounding cord connected from your tailbone down, down into the centre of the earth. You could visualize a tree trunk running from your spine deep into the earth.

Imagine the energy block is now loose and ready to fall down the tree trunk away from you. Down, down, down and away.

Allow any thoughts or feelings that say, "This is stupid." Or "I don't believe it." Or "Ya, but, I can't just let her opinion slide away so easily!"

Allow those thoughts to flow down and away in the same way you gave that energetic block more space. Let those thoughts slide down the grounding cord or tree trunk. Gravity will draw them away from you.

If more blocks show up from other people in your life, allow those to slide down. Keep doing this until you feel complete.

Great job today!

Chapter Three

DAY 3: REPITITION & VISUALIZATION

Whenever you feel overwhelmed or uncomfortable about a situation, create a success mantra for yourself. Then repeat it often.

Repeating creates a "wave" of vibration of energy around you. When said often enough it becomes a new belief. This process is used to amplify and magnetize the results you are looking for.

Thoughts that have a certainty and charge to them, become the habits and patterns in your thinking. When mixed in with your feelings, they become the "glue" which attracts other similar or related thoughts. And then you can't stop thinking about the stuff that has an energetic charge.

The good thoughts will increase your level of joy. But when those bad thoughts drag you down, it seems you can't let them go. This exercise will help.

This process works and you will learn to control and use it to your advantage.

Creating and then saying your mantra out loud

creates a vibration of energy that generates a greater sense of confidence.

Try this mantra. Read it out loud:

"I here and now promise by creating in my mind a clear mental picture (fill in the blank for confidence or success or anything else you want to manifest), I will devote ten minutes daily and allow (fill in the blank for confidence or success or other thing) to come into my life. I'll never stop trying until it's here. This or something better."

ACTION STEP

Think of a situation you really want to have occur in your life. Maybe you've always dreamed about visiting another country. Maybe you want to be a professional photographer. You want a new car or a new home. You want to be married, or pregnant. You just want to lose some weight and feel better about yourself. You definitely want more financial support and reduce your debts!

Grab a pen and use the page at the end of this chapter to write your thoughts.

Find a comfortable chair, sit upright, feet flat on the floor, hands in your lap. Breathe in and as you exhale, imagine your whole body relaxing.

Repeat deep breaths until you feel calm.

Keep your eyes closed and imagine that you are sitting in front of large blank movie or TV screen. See yourself in the movie. You are working or playing or completing the project you want to accomplish. See yourself involved in the situation you really want to have occurring in your life.

Now imagine you are being given a bonus cheque for your project. Or you are going out on a date with the person you want to love and be loved back, or you are receiving a diploma for your education completion. You see and feel yourself twenty pounds lighter. You see and hear, and feel yourself as you've made it. You've succeeded in receiving what you want. Woo-hoo! You did it!

Pay attention to all the details, how you look, how you feel, where you are and who is with you. Notice your emotions and your feelings. When this image feels complete, allow yourself to get present, breathe and open your eyes.

Immediately write down what you saw and felt. Read it often. This is your visualization you will refer to over and over until you have achieved your success.

Tell yourself every day that you deserve this new imagining.

Great job today!

Chapter Four

DAY 4: ATTITUDE ADJUSTMENTS

And then there's attitude. Attitude is simply a conscious choice that drives your physical learning and behaviors. For example, you can choose to follow up on opportunities and you can choose not to. When you tell yourself not to follow up because ...

- you don't want to seem pushy
- you're too busy
- it's too hard to get dressed and go out
- you're not sure what to say
- you're afraid of getting rejected.

It's attitude that takes over.

In a study done by the Harvard Business School, results showed that top salespeople and producers:

- don't take "no" personally
- accept 100% responsibility for their results

- they don't blame the economy, competition, product
- they spend the bulk of their time on priorities
- they put themselves in their customers' shoes
- are self-disciplined and persistent
- are honest with themselves and the customer.

How many of the above elements could you relate to?

Now it's time to examine your old notions and bring awareness to them. Awareness may be all you need to dissolve an old pattern or belief.

First, ask yourself, why would you want to heal them?

If you're struggling making basic ends meet, you might want to heal a pattern that keeps you from earning more or spending less.

If you're constantly fighting with the very person you love, you might want to heal a pattern that keeps you from enjoying their company.

If you're sick and tired, you might want to heal a pattern that keeps you from being healthy and vibrant.

ACTION STEP

On the notes page at the end of this chapter, write your list of old fears and beliefs.

Now examine this list and decide if they are true for you right now.

Replace any of these with positive statements or affirmations that resonate as true for you. For example if you've been repeating "I'm a failure at everything!"

replace it with "I am successful in these areas in my life (fill in the blank)."

With each item you became aware of, ask yourself how true are they right now. It's time to look at that belief and decide once and for all if it's serving you or hindering you. It can be that simple.

Great job today!

Chapter Five

DAY 5: TRANSFORM WORRY INTO HAPPY

How are you doing today? Are any pesky fears or thoughts of worry coming up for you?

Up to now you probably didn't want them surfacing. It's time to view them a little differently. Now when they come up, acknowledge them. Yes, you could even say, "Well hello there!" They are the clues to the next steps you will take to clear them out.

Write them out on the page after this chapter. Stuff will come up because you are already shifting your energy. And loosened energy needs to be free.

Like a new pair of shoes. At first they're tight and hurt your feet. Eventually you stretch them out and finally, they are so expanded, they flip and fall off. That's what can happen to a belief!

What if a really big issue is coming up for you?

Ask yourself what you are "really" worrying about?

What are you afraid will happen? What's the worst that can happen?

Once you become aware of the fear, it begins to have less energy. So don't dwell on it. Instead give it space. Give it room.

For example, you are worried about having enough money to pay your rent. You are afraid your roommate will accuse you of not carrying your fair share of the load. You're afraid he or she will scream at you or worse, ignore you and dislike you!

ACTION STEP

Whatever issue is worrying you, use this exercise to stop it and reverse the energy flow. Loosen the tightness so it falls away.

If you need to relax more, sit in a comfortable chair, breathe, and imagine the large screen in front of you. Imagine this new scene right here and right now where ever you are.

See yourself writing the cheque and handing it to your roommate. Also imagine that you have extra cash in your pocket or purse. Imagine you are saying out loud, "Wow, how silly of me to worry because the money flows easily into my bank account. And my roommate respects me and likes me!"

See your roommate smile and appreciate you.

Say "thank you" out loud and any other forms of gratitude you feel comfortable expressing.

Feel the energy of relief over your ability to pay your rent, have cash left over and getting a huge hug from your roommate.

Please remember, use all your senses when using

your imagination. See it, hear it, smell it, taste it, think about it, feel it, and appreciate it. And use your gut instinct to truly believe this process works. Now you're using intuition the way it is meant to be used.

This exercise will change your state of mind and magnetize the desired outcome for you. Feeling better is the primary step. The next steps will show up.

Great job today!

Chapter Six

DAY 6: CHANGE HAPPENS

If you're like me, you can't wait for something to happen right now.

The thought of change or acquiring what we want taking months and years can feel devastating. If we get too disillusioned about our results, we fall back into old patterns and habits.

A habit is simply a behavior that's repeated over and over until it becomes an integral part of who we are and how we do things. Habits could become our masters if we allow them. We can become slaves to habits and they work against us but only if we allow them.

One such debilitating habit is procrastination. A lot has been written about procrastination. And I'm sure you've reminded yourself over and over about how you "must" get things done.

Procrastination occurs when those justifying thoughts creep in and convince you of the dire need to put things off. So how can you catch those thoughts?

Before we go into the action step, here's an example.

A client of mine wanted to write a book. She knew the value of becoming an author. It would certainly increase her exposure and bring in more income. But she postponed the project for years. When I asked her why, she said she didn't have time because she travelled and when she was home, her focus was her family.

I asked her why she didn't write when she was away.

She said she was tired after travelling and meetings.

I asked her why she didn't get up a little earlier and write.

She asked me why I was so intent on her writing a book!

We laughed.

She realized what she just said and sheepishly admitted she was stuck in being stuck.

After all, she realized she did want to write a book, however, she fell into the habit of using excuses as obstacles to getting started.

For her, she was finally heard and that set a different intention for her. Hopefully you have someone who hears you if you can't quite grasp your own thoughts. Say them out loud.

Procrastination can be very, very tricky.

The following action step is designed to ground and reduce the procrastination energy that seems to take over whenever a project looms.

ACTION STEP

Let's start with an easy meditative exercise which will become your new every day morning habit.

Find a comfortable chair and quiet space. Receive a few deep breaths and scan your body. How are you doing right now?

Call your energy into the center of your head. Imagine that the centre of your head is clean and spacious. Open into the stillness or the light there. Clean out the center of your head with a golden sponge.

Now imagine a column of gold falling from about fifteen feet above your head. Connect in with that gold (like your personal sunshine). Bring it through your entire body.

Put down a grounding cord. You did this in a previous day. Connect an energetic stream or imagine it a tree trunk or whatever works for you, from your tail bone to the center of the earth. Allow energies that no longer serve you to drop down that cord. Allow gravity to do its work.

Fill up the space inside and around you with gold.

Open your eyes. Breathe into what it would be like to have this practice be part of your life (visualize it).

Using these tools will help you instantly access information in your life and having a meditation practice will support you staying grounded and feeling loved.

Now more new habits can include:

- Restrict TV, telephone, video, web, social media time and use them as rewards for completion of important tasks.
- Write, read, sew, study, or whatever activity requires your attention for completion, in a quiet area free of distractions.

- Put up a Do Not Disturb sign to show your kids, spouse and friends you value your time alone.
- Restructure your time with work and play to gain the most time advantages to complete projects.
- Get an accountability partner, someone who will support you in recognizing and releasing bad habits, someone who will not save you but serve you to move through this! You know who they are!

Chapter Seven

DAY 7: A WEEK OF CREATIVITY

*L*et's recap so far.

You must have a clear vision of what you want to accomplish and with whom. And it's not just "because" you desire something. Your vision must be so clear it feels as if it's real to you.

You must have a support network in place you can consult with and mastermind with. But the caution here is that you must surround yourself with people who are at your level of support, love, confidence and growth.

An interesting little story here. A client shared he was going to get marketing support from his friend to help him spread the word about his new business. But his friend was unemployed, in the middle of a divorce, drinking heavily and not such a good choice. You see, you need to be careful who you surround yourself with. Energy is very important.

This brings us to this next bit. Find someone like a relevant mentor, coach or friend who will tell you the truth.

Your mentor will tell you if you're on the right track and will gently (or not so gently if necessary) stop you from making the same mistakes. Don't get me wrong. Someone else doesn't know what will work best for you. However, sometimes looking at a decision or situation from the outside in with fresh eyes can reveal hidden clues to the next step.

Finally, you must be persistent and willing to go the full mile to reach success. That means encouragement and a little ass-kicking if necessary to take action!

But ...

What I discovered was that even if you followed all the criteria above, took action daily, were determined to make a success of your life, it could still fall apart in surprising ways that keep you dumbfounded! You keep wondering why it doesn't work!

You see, what's missing here is the need for more clearing of that mental context (beliefs) you hold about yourself and other people.

What causes most distress is ignoring that inner critic that talks and talks and whimpers and cries at you day and night, "You can't do it, can ya! You're a loser! You'll never make it!"

You've given that voice the power over your life choices and now what? You believe the stuff of that little voice. However, it's not your fault. You picked it up most of it without evening knowing. Remember 90/10 rule in Day 2?

So what are these dirty little secrets of programming in your mind and what can you do about them?

Can you tell the difference right now if your mind

chatter encourages you to step out and live bigger or does it squash and crash your dreams? Does it encourage you to take action or hide out in fear?

ACTION STEP

Become aware. Here's what to notice first.

How you interact with people at home is how you interact everywhere else, including work.

How you interact in personal relationships is how you interact in other relationships.

How you believe you are is how others perceive you!

Ouch. Now that came out of left field didn't it?

If you believe you're not worthy or not talented, or heaven forbid, not loved, people tend to pick up on that energy and respond appropriately.

What do I mean? For example people may seem to shut you out without you or their knowing why. And that's because *you* believe you're not good enough to be included. *You* believe you are flawed in some way!

It took me a long time to figure out that when I thought I was protecting myself from people invalidating me, that energetic invisible shield kept people away from me. Even the ones I needed to help me grow and succeed!

See what I mean? They act around you the way you expect them to from the inside out. The trouble comes when you do not know consciously you are doing this.

So if you become aware of the way you think about yourself, you would become aware of why people treat you the way they do. That includes potential clients and lovers alike!

Another example is if you hang around negative people who are doom and gloom sayers about economy and getting shafted instead of focusing on the successes, you stand a good chance of failing. Your energy becomes negative as well.

If you're too occupied with planning, gathering, researching and more gathering, planning and researching, you stop yourself from doing what you originally wanted to do! Results don't come from just planning and gathering. They come from taking action to achieve the goals you set out. Are you taking action even if you don't really feel you're ready?

The trick is to become aware of what you are telling yourself about how soon you "should" get started. Then you can easily shift into action.

Great job today!

Chapter Eight

DAY 8: VALIDATION

If your outer interpretation of people and situations no longer supports and enhances you, then the place to look is inside.

Can you imagine for a moment that you sense a potential within you, unrealized and curious as to why you can't reach your full potential worth in money and appreciation?

Can you also imagine how often you worry about disappointing your family, yourself and your clients about achieving the best results for all?

You may be hiding out, or you may be afraid to admit you have reached your "success ceiling". You know that upper limit like a glass ceiling you can't seem to surpass? Like never getting more than minimum wage? Or never getting past first base?

If you feel frustrated as you read these, then you are on the edge of a revelation and ready to make a change that will remove the "success ceiling" once and for all.

When you find the core belief that stops you from

expanding financially, intellectually and emotionally, you will inevitably affect all the people around you.

For instance, a vision for a successful and lucrative business is not enough. That vision can't come into form without action. But here's the thing. The actions won't bring real results unless you've cleared the blocks by doing the inner work!

The inner block or blocks are stuck unless you experience a level of validation and empowerment as well as satisfaction that you're telling yourself the truth.

One big challenge is to validate yourself along the way. How easy or difficult is it for you to say to yourself, "Hey buddy, you're the best!" Keep telling yourself you're doing a great job!

ACTION STEP

Validate, validate, validate! If you don't experience authentic validation for who you are and what you offer, no one else will either!

Today, acknowledge yourself for absolutely everything you've done and for absolutely everything you haven't done. That's right, for everything today! Practice validating yourself until you become tired of yourself.

Give yourself a woo-hoo for getting up ten minutes earlier and riding that stationary bike for five more minutes. Pat yourself on the back for window shopping without spending a dime for something you don't need. Congratulate yourself for ordering the chef's salad instead of the fries and gravy.

Good job! And now, validate some more!

Give yourself a silent thank you for daring to introduce yourself to that new guy or gal in the neighborhood. Smile because you picked up the phone to contact a new client.

Here's the most important thing you will ever apply:

"Treat yourself the way you want to be treated!"

Chapter Nine

DAY 9: RELATIONSHIP FACTOR

You decided on the ideal career or love interest, and now you want to build the relationship.

You bravely faced and released some of your biggest relationship issues. You became aware of distorted thoughts from your past and even bust through long time habits. You're ready to begin to build.

But if you make this critical relationship judgment (to yourself or out loud) your chances of long-term business or personal relationship success will fizzle just as sure as the light flickers out in a burnt spotlight!

Before I tell you what it is, let me share this story.

A client had a growing concern that as her career skyrocketed, she would spend less and less time with her family.

She became so concerned that her energy felt heavy. She hung out in a state of hopeful denial. She hoped she was valued and denied that her spouse or children would be angry and disappointed instead of happy for her.

Then the inevitable happened. Prospects didn't want to work with her. Why? They actually felt her heavy energy and chose not to hire her. The energy was all wrong.

Here's what she failed to do: *ask herself why she's really in business, and what does her family as well as her client base expect?*

SHE HELD onto beliefs that mirrored she wasn't quite good enough. She experienced difficulty, frustrations and lack of interest from her family and clients. Why? Because instead of eliminating doubt about having a business, she proceeded with hidden agenda that she would be unsupported. She continued to worry that her family would not understand her ambition.

You may have experienced something similar, but you know what?

You can get past this and actually increase business and increase family time.

ACTION STEP

At the beginning stage of your business development, or even well into the success phases, ask questions of your partners, family members and friends who may be involved and affected by your success (or lack of). You could communicate with those who support you and get a real sense of what genuine support feels like. Then you release the doubt to continue feeling good about your decisions.

You do the same with the people you think don't support you. You hear what they have to offer, remove your own doubts and continue in the direction that feels best for you.

Once you "hear" what the important people in your life have to say, you won't go into assuming what they might say!

You are not an island onto yourself. And one of the biggest mistakes new entrepreneurs make is not asking for support from relevant resources. Instead they assume what may or may not come as perceived support.

They also fail to prepare themselves by:

- taking proactive steps
- keeping an inspired vision of their business and life choice and make goal and action adjustments to meet that vision.
- become more aware of everyone's options and opinions (realize they are not totally clear on their own picture of success)
- understanding what the industry expects
- understand what the best and worst outcomes could be
- and becoming so crystal clear about who their client is and what they want.

See what I mean? *It's your expectations* of yourself in business and in personal relationships that require a thorough investigation and not controlling and manipulating anyone to fit into a routine that just ain't goin' to happen!

You could let go of expectations and actually live in the moment. Sounds weird, doesn't it?

This is your chance to concentrate on and *make a habit of taking care of yourself first*—and let go of any expectations of how to get there.

Here's what else you can immediately apply to help yourself stay sane, appreciated and in demand.

First develop a positive energetic relationship with yourself. That means find out what you believe about yourself and then decide to like yourself anyway. Or would you prefer not to have met yourself?

I didn't think so.

You could consider who you respect and emulate them.

Spend at least a day a week devoted to doing the things you love. People devote time and attention to things outside of themselves such as work, family and community. Where in that mix do you care for yourself?

Just applying these small actions will net surprising results. You'll begin to see many more opportunities to enjoy time with yourself.

Write it down. Journal your findings. Use the page at the end of this chapter.

Great job today!

Chapter Ten

DAY 10: LIFE IS YOUR MIRROR

Your mood is upbeat and you are proud that you got that contract or an extended project from a current client.

You're happy your kids are well and safe. Then someone cuts you off on the highway!

How do you react? Because your energy feels good, you don't react negatively. You might just shrug your shoulders and keep driving with a smile on your face.

Another day, you feel somber and want to hide out.

Your spouse growls at you as you walk into the room.

You ask yourself "What now and why me?"

Now if you were in your car and someone cut you off, how would you feel about it?

A whole lot different you would imagine.

So here's where the rubber meets the road. The truth is, the world shows up for you according to your beliefs and how you feel about them in any given moment.

Instead of blaming the world, ask yourself, what **is in**

you that is creating your responses about what is showing up?

You are not normally a sad or growly person. It's what you do (or don't) that creates the sadness. It's what you think (or don't) that creates the melancholy. It's not your client and it's not your kids!

Bear with me. We're on a journey of discovery and you're very close to finding out what makes you tick.

Beliefs run you. You may not even be aware of what they are. So it's important to be aware of what you think about throughout your awareness journey.

Let me ask you this. Do you find yourself complaining?

Or feeling overwhelmed?

Or why do they have to change their minds so much?

Or that decision-maker doesn't know what he's doing?

Or worse yet, do you have the habit of telling others what hasn't gone right or the way you expected?

Complaining is an addictive habit. Complaining creates neural pathways and circuits in the brain that look for more things to complain about. Complaining literally feeds on your positive energy and *sucks the joy, profits and success out of your life.*

So why do so many of us focus on what we don't want?

To a degree it's healthy because then you can eliminate those and focus on getting what you do want. But not everyone does that.

Because we're programmed by the media, society and

our family to moan and groan about how awful things are we are accustomed to complaining.

ACTION STEP

Grab that pen. On the last page of this chapter, write down your most popular complaints. That means listening to your brain chatter.

Notice how you respond when your client asks you to change something you've just done. Notice what pops into your head when he tells you he's not going to pay you for things he didn't ask for.

Notice what you tell yourself when your partner changes plans?

Check if others around you are complaining and how you feel when you hear them complain. Have you now become a nuisance complainer yourself?

Take note of how, who and how long you talk to others who complain. Remember that how you spend your time is how you spend your life.

Notice if you're talking about what you want or what you don't want. Life is your mirror. Life is a reflection of what you think and believe. It's in the energy that surrounds you. It shows you if you're stuck or flowing.

I love this metaphor for reflection which I call "Annie Get Your Gun!"

Notice that every time you point your finger and either accuse, blame or even positively "point out" something, only ONE finger is out there? The rest point BACK to you.

That's how reflection works.

ACTION STEP

Pick one day a week when you could spend completely for yourself. Challenge yourself to become aware of your thoughts and words. Catch yourself complaining and stop it. Continue to validate yourself at every chance you can. Notice how you feel at the end of the day.

Journal and then have a good night's sleep.

Great job today!

Chapter Eleven

DAY 11: TAP INTO YOUR POWER

When you stop blaming prospects for not hiring you, or stop blaming the whole world for you not achieving as much as you hoped, you shift and release that energy. You start to expand into what you really want, and you get what you want.

You get clarity about what is most important to you. You get vision.

ACTION STEPS

Here are a few ways to develop vision.

- Be yourself. Trust yourself.
- Work and love strongly.
- Make your business such a safe place that you never experience failure or invalidation.
- If you make a mistake, try again.

- Ask for people's opinions and then, don't run your life on people's opinions—run it on your own desires. Trust your intuition and gut.
- Know what you don't want. But then, turn it around and know what you do want. You will achieve it without invalidating who you are.
- Ask yourself over and over, what else does this mean? What else do you think? Especially if you're afraid. That's when you get the greatest understanding that you can make your life and your love of business work well for you.
- Now write it down. Write an imaginary scenario of your perfect business day. Make it as clear as you possibly can.
- If the day is not coming out as clearly and vibrantly as you want, go to the last page of this chapter and write a brief plan of what you want to accomplish. Don't forget details such as where you sit, what color are your walls, who are you talking to, who are you writing for, and how much are you receiving in joy and money and so on. Then write some action steps to get there.

KEEP GOING. You're doing a great job! And remember, always ask yourself why you want to achieve what you want. The answers come. The answers spur on more imagination and clarity.

ACTION STEP

Here's another powerful way of creating an intention to support having a best day on a regular basis.

Imagine a clear bubble in front of you. Allow a stream of golden light to fill it from the top. Now imagine that the bubble is connected to another stream attached to the bottom and grounded all the way down into the center of the earth.

Imagine what you would enjoy as an intention today. You could imagine releasing your need to over eat. You could ask for a goal to complete itself by the end of the day. Whatever you want, put that thought into the bubble.

Now add some support energy like the intention to manifest with ease, grace, love, and fun. Next, add the thought, "this or something better".

Finally, release the grounding cord below and allow the bubble with the intention to zoom out into the universe. Stop thinking about it, and trust that your intention shall come to you fulfilled.

Great job today!

Chapter Twelve

DAY 12: VISION MASTERY

It wasn't that long ago that I had a panicky feeling in the pit of my stomach. I was wondering how the heck I was ever going to get clients, make money and pay back the debt I incurred with courses and trainings.

Time and costs included marketing, website creation, monthly fees, business cards, a bit of advertising, networking... well you know the drill. And that didn't include my valuable time and effort at home washing dishes, clothes, dusting and eating!

I thought I was doing a lot, but I was oblivious to why each day was such a struggle.

I was focused on achieving goals. I was obsessed with single-minded intentions. I was lost in details and forgot the most significant principle, my vision!

Let me explain.

I've had a lifelong vision: to significantly influence people to understand and become aware that when they are conscious (mindful) of what they think, they are in control of their life outcomes.

I've practiced this vision with my mom for decades. She used to say things like, "Oh if only it would stay dry for one more week so we can get the crops off, then I'll be happy." So she was a curmudgeon for the rest of the week worried if it would rain or not. Then she said things like, "Well when you get as old as me, you won't remember things either."

I got wild with her. I ask her to stop saying those things. I wondered why she is so intent on forecasting doom.

Because she planned her life with daily and weekly goals living season to season on a farm, she's in the habit of continuing in this manner. When she was living in a seniors' home, she had plans on a meal-to-meal basis, which she can walk back from her room to the next snack. Her attention was "why me" when she ached in pain (past) and "why aren't my kids visiting me" (future) when she felt lonely. She gone now, but over the years we could tell she didn't have a compelling vision for the duration of her life.

The main issue was that my father passed a decade ago and she hadn't decided what to do with the rest of her life. Instead, she mourned him the entire time until she went to meet him in heaven.

Her immediate goals were being met, however, vision in this case, was completely missing.

Compelling visions keep life interesting.

Set the larger vision and the smaller goals continue to lead to the whole.

Goals are just a way to further your vision and not an end in themselves.

If you keep this in mind, you won't get stuck. In fact, the problem with just having goals is that if you set a goal, you actually focus on its completion and miss opportunities that come along which may be relevant to the bigger picture.

You already know from previous chapters that what you focus on takes all your attention and energy. However, a vision is long-term, purposeful, and allows openness to possibilities.

Goals also keep you in the past (you made a goal last year and still remind yourself of it) and in the future (you complete a goal and strive to decide what's next).

But the power is in the present.

Goals and strategies force you to stay in the past and the future. They inhibit every one of us from living in the present.

So let's envision first.

I discovered that if I tapped into the day itself, allow it to reflect back to me what was really going on, and dig to find out what was actually preventing me from advancing, I became present and encouraged.

With a to-the-point, direct approach, you can find out for yourself exactly what keeps you from achieving more.

You could have a simple system to figure out what's been going on with what you've been doing all these years, change it, and go on to make the next segment of your life absolutely resistance free and successful.

ACTION STEP

Here's the next big clue to discovering your vision.

Become really aware of what is happening for you!

Once you become aware of your surroundings, you get real clues as to what inspires you and what is creating success for you. You'll also see what's getting in your way.

When you become fully aware, you take full responsibility for your results, and you can find out what keeps you motivated and what scares you.

Today, notice everything. Notice how you act and react. Notice how others act and react. Notice everything!

Your vision comes out of this observation.

ANOTHER ACTION STEP

You must understand your true desires and not the ones you think other people will recognize and see in you. What are your "true" wants? Decide right now that you have a vision for yourself for your life. Then goals and details will support that vision.

Grab a pen and use the page at the end of this chapter. I'll give you an example first. Here's one that fascinates many people: adventure. Your vision will be different, obviously. Let's see how to develop a goal that will support this vision.

Draw a chart for yourself with seven rows. In the first row, write your most pressing goal or wish. See this diagram on the page here as an example.

1. Goal/wish	Money
2. What will I do? Why do I want it?	Money to go on a vacation without taking out a loan to pay for it.
3. Reason I want this goal.	I want to go on vacation and enjoy ourselves without worrying or skimping.
4. Rewrite goal as final	What I really want is to go on a vacation.
5. Specific details of goal.	The vacation will be to Greece and the Mediterranean 5 star and 1st class.
6. Restate goal as an intention.	I intend to manifest a 1st class vacation with all the 5 star treatment to go with it!
7. State the emotions I feel as well as the certainty I now have I created this goal.	I feel so excited and happy, relaxed and at ease knowing this vacation has already come to me, so now I am waiting for it to arrive!

In the second row, ask yourself, why do you want this goal? You're always asking the question, "Why?"

Write the answer in the second row.

In the third row, rewrite the goal to in include the reason you wanted this goal from row two.

Now look at this new expanded goal and ask yourself again, why? Why do you want this goal?

Write your answer in the fourth row as your final goal.

In the fifth row, include some specific details about the reworked goal.

In the sixth row, restate your goal as an intention in the present tense.

Finally, in the last row, state how this will make you feel and make it the declaration that you have already created your goal. Add your emotions such as ease, fun, grace, love, and so on.

Reword and formulate your goals so they best suit what you are "really" seeking. Asking for money is okay. However, the goal you want may come to you in different ways that you don't even know right now! So don't close up your options!

Now, repeat after me: It's okay to feel good. It's okay to have what I really want. In fact, it's okay to feel good all of the time!

If you disagree with this, you likely hit your "success ceiling" (you know that glass ceiling that bumps you back down as you're climbing to success).

Here's another way of releasing a stuck goal. Goals only become completed when you make the commitment to achieving them, no matter what! Ask yourself if you're committed to the goal. Then it frees itself to unfold with your intended actions.

Great job today!

Chapter Thirteen

DAY 13: TIME MASTERY

Getting started on the path to increased health, or wealth and other personal satisfaction seems overwhelming because we don't know where to start.

We've created so many barriers by allowing beliefs that are just not true to grow more than we really intended.

For some it's a surprise how little has been accomplished. For others, that fear gets in the way of doing even the smallest action. Doing regular exercise, getting a better job, working for yourself, advertise, ask for the order, and receive the abundance that is your true essence and rightful purpose in life can seem daunting.

But sometimes we don't know which one to tear down first.

In the end, it doesn't matter which one. All roads lead to Rome, so to speak.

Removing any block will start empowering you and

building your confidence. Then with greater confidence you will feel ready, willing and able to tackle more.

The one thing I hear most often is that people don't have enough time.

Whatever the belief, one thing to remember is that you created it. So if you had the power to remind yourself over and over that you don't have enough time, you have the power to tear that down.

Work, school and home. They all demand a minimum of time each. And the more responsibility you place on yourself, the less time appears to support you giving it to all those areas.

Don't despair, there is help. Of course there are the all the regular suggestions like learning to prioritize and manage activities.

There are time log tools where you set up activity plans, and the popular daily planners to help you keep on time and on track.

Today you can write appointments and have your cell phones and electronic devices beep and click to remind you of your next sessions and so on.

But you have to develop the habit of putting the information into the device or write it into the planner. Then you have to remember to carry those things with you all the time. What's more, you have to remember to leave time for yourself for emergencies and the unexpected!

Are you organized or willing to be organized enough to plan your life on your cell phone and/or planner?

I didn't think so. That task is a difficult one at best. Few people enjoy the planning and noting of activities. Most fly by the seat of their pants.

So what to do? What I'm about to share is unusual, surprisingly effective and weird all at the same time! So remember your Day one task? Keep an open mind.

ACTION STEP

Live in Einstein Time.

When you shift into Einstein Time you develop a harmonious relationship with time, "You are where time comes from." Let me explain further.

Old paradigm: The common and Newtonian view says there's only a finite amount of time, and it must be portioned out so there will be enough of it to do the things we need to do in a day, a week or even a lifetime. (Scarcity) leads to uncomfortable feelings of time urgency. You'll either have too little or too much time. The illusion is that time is out there.

New paradigm: Einstein Time, proven by Albert himself, states that time is in you and you decide how long or short of time you need to complete a task.

For example, when an hour with your beloved feels like a minute. A minute on a hot stove feels like an hour, you expanded or contracted time within you to experience this. You didn't even know it.

Awareness: contracting and anxiety produces a sense of time slowing down. Instead, flow from the inside out, think from the inside out, and take full ownership of time.

So quit thinking time is out there. It's not. You make time. Now it's up to you to take ownership and when you do, time will stop owning you.

If you don't have enough time, ask yourself these questions "Where in my life am I not taking full ownership? Or what am I trying to disown? Or in what aspect of my life do I need to take full or more responsibility?

Stress and conflict are caused by resisting acceptance and ownership of time.

How to begin: There is only one way. Stop complaining about time. Here are common lies we say to ourselves:

- I wish I had time to stop and chat, but I'm in a hurry.
- Where did the time go?
- There simply aren't enough hours in the day.
- Love to talk, but I've gotta run.
- I have to get to the bank.
- *I don't have time to do that right now.* Now come on, would you stop whatever you are doing to help a hurt child? Of course you would. So really you decide on the circumstances yourself, you see?

And because everything is energy, notice where "not enough time" feels like pressure within your body. Let it go.

Great job today!

Chapter Fourteen

DAY 14: MEMORY & BELIEF MASTERY

> *"No memory is ever alone; it's at the end of a trail of memories, a dozen trails that each have their own associations."*
>
> — LOUIS L'AMOUR (RIDE THE RIVER)

Sure we have computers and electronic devices to remind ourselves about anything. However, our memory serves us as a powerful processor. When we receive or take information, we decide whether to store it, discard it or reformulate it into perception. Hence our beliefs come out of that memory function.

Yes, that's how beliefs are formed. A belief is an information that is held and even altered to suit ourselves at the time we gathered it.

Retention is the storing of data. All the data needs to move quickly from our short term memory to long term memory in order to retain it. What else happens is, we forget about it after a while and then it becomes unconscious.

The trouble with unconsciously retained data is that if it's negative, it continues to run our lives. The good news is, so does the positive.

Recall is how we bring back or remember what was learned, believed or stored.

Recalling can be challenging or simple. It depends on the energetic charge the data or memory has. If you don't want to look at something, you won't. That's where the decision comes in. You decide whether you want to remember something or block it out.

So how does the data become unconscious? Repetition, repetition, repetition!

The process goes like this: you experience a situation by either feeling good about it or feeling bad. Then you begin to process that data in your thoughts and make a decision whether it's true or a lie you're telling yourself. Finally, you talk about it, dream about it, confirm its validity, and voila, it becomes believable.

Now you have committed to believing it, and it starts to show up in your life. That's the power of the universal law of attraction. Simple as that.

If the belief doesn't serve you, the next step is to figure out when you formed it.

A common belief struggling entrepreneurs repeat consciously and unconsciously is that "People with money somehow deserve it ... and I don't."

Yet people try to demystify money by saying that it's just "a neutral instrument for facilitating the exchange of goods and services." Like Monopoly money.

Somehow, that's supposed to help you to let go of the emotional baggage you've attached to money and change your mind about whether you should or shouldn't have more. It won't. But here's what will.

What busts this belief actually goes back to something much more basic: take a closer look at the source. What's the source? Your story.

ACTION STEP

Grab the pen and get ready to write. First begin to write the answers to these questions: Who's the authority in your past who wrote the rules of who wins in the game of having money or not? Have you ever seen any rules? Or have you just carried forward a bunch of hearsay from childhood that you never thought to question?

Maybe they told you that you weren't worthy of having more than someone else or more than they had.

Were you told you were not being "worthy of"? Ha! Be brave and tell yourself your story and then we're going to settle this argument once and for all.

What I'm also suggesting is be vulnerable here. Open up and admit (to yourself) which event triggered the most damage to your esteem.

Now I want you to think of a time when you were disappointed, hurt, or worse, disillusioned about your own power and ability to make a difference in your life.

Take a few moments and remember that incident.

. . .

Our beliefs became established at a very early age. For most of us, when we get a belief like "I'm not good enough" it comes from interacting with our parents or primary caregiver when we were small.

But a word of caution here. Discovering that "I'm not good enough" coming from parents does not give any of us permission to blame them.

In fact, most parents did their very best with us. And they loved us. They played out what they knew and how to do it from their own experiences as children with their parents.

What parents don't realize is that children (including themselves) were forming beliefs all along.

No one really had much training. They just didn't realize the impact they had on children. Most didn't intend any harm at all.

This next statement is general.

Parents want their children to be obedient, and children want to explore.

Even though it's a core judgment about raising children, stuff happens anyway.

You may have experienced something like this. You may not have done what your parents wanted you to do. So they looked annoyed, said nothing, or said a lot. Whatever happened, you took their signals as a reaction to their not liking your actions.

Now you may not have experienced the trauma I did with my father, but you may have experienced a situation or incident that could have made you believe that you were not good enough.

The criticism could be subtle or harsh. What is your story?

Now what if you can't remember an incident that could have triggered "I'm not good enough?" No matter.

You don't need to remember a specific incident. But you do remember their reaction. That's all you need to remember to set the belief in motion.

Once you realize that there are no rules about who should and shouldn't have money, and many people who are dishonorable (hence, unworthy) have money, this myth has been busted.

We're coming to that and more.

Shelves of books have been written on the role of self-worth, fear, blame, guilt, and shame in people's unwillingness to know where they stand financially, emotionally, in business and personal relationships.

I won't go into all the details here, but I can assure you that everyone I've worked with has told me (once they were willing to get honest about their real story) that it was never as bad as they had imagined.

It never is. When we don't know, we imagine the absolute worst. And, somehow, by knowing the real reasons behind the fears, those fears suddenly hold far less power over you. They become just situations.

Write your story and become aware of its energy. Then let it go. Soften the impact it's had on you over the years.

Great job today!

Chapter Fifteen

DAY 15: FORGIVENESS MASTERY

To forgive is to give back to God. If you don't like the word God, use eternal essence, spirit, or whichever concept you believe would work best for you.

It's not about being correct with universal principles. It's all about how to rid the pain and anguish you experience when you think about something or someone who has slighted you.

This tool is worth a million dollars and more. You get it for the price of this powerful book. Congratulations!

Now this tool is yours right now to make huge shifts for your own peace of mind and well-being. Are you game?

Bubbles. Yes, bubbles are the forgiveness tools that do all the work for you!

All you have to do is give up the tainted thought or energy block and let the bubble do the rest!

ACTION STEP

Find a quiet space and sit upright in a chair.

Close your eyes, take a deep breath, and allow it to filter throughout your body.

See a transparent rose out in front of you. Let this rose represent yourself.

Make a wish about how you want to change a relationship or get closure, or whatever you need that has been difficult up to now to forgive. Now drop it into the rose. Here's how you will read that rose about yourself.

FLOWER: First set your intention that you are going to get your answers. Ask the flower head "What do you need to do in your life to release the hold someone else had on you?" The flower will send you words, feelings, imagines or messages that you need to know. Talk aloud for 2 minutes.

Just start talking out loud about what you see. If you see a color, what does the color mean? Is there any energy that would prevent you from letting this pain go? Any dark patches? What do they mean? Keep talking out loud for another minute or so.

STEM: Now read the stem. Similarly, ask the stem for answers to these types of questions. "What is your joy, closure or peace of mind grounded to?" "What is the energy that would prevent your joy, closure or peace of mind grounded to?" Talk out loud to yourself for at least two minutes. Good job.

LEAVES: Now read the leaves on the left side of your rose. Ask things like, "How will your forgiveness and peace of mind affect others?"

Now read the leaves on the right. Ask, "How will your forgiveness and peace of mind affect you?" Just keep asking for the information and keep talking out loud to yourself. Take at least two minutes or more per side.

You are learning a valuable skill here. Sometimes it will feel easy, sometimes it will feel hard, but validate yourself in the process of learning this SKILL. Reading a rose showing your essence is natural and everyone has the ability to do this. Your essence shows up and all you have to do is reclaim your power.

Here's where it gets really slick and effective.

Imagine a bubble out in front of you that has a powerful magnet inside. Allow the magnet to pull out the undesirable energy that prevents you from forgiving. You can even allow the magnet to pull the rose up into it.

Include everything you saw so far. The situation, the person, your feelings, your pain. Allow the magnet to "swoosh" all the energy into it. Now swoosh that rose into the bubble.

Next put a second bubble beside the first. In it is another very powerful magnet. Allow this second magnet to draw all your special and loving energy out of the first bubble. Allow the second magnet to pull your power back from the person, situation or issue out of the first bubble. You want to draw back all the power you put into that first bubble. Now pop the first bubble and let it go.

Take the second bubble and bring it into you. Pop it inside you wherever you wish. Allow your power to saturate throughout your entire body. Ahhh. Let the positive energy flow inside and welcome it. Validate yourself for an energetic shift well done. Great job today!

Chapter Sixteen

DAY 16: WORTHINESS MASTERY

Some of you may be saying, "Yeah, but my beliefs around hurtful persons, or money, or other relationships are part of my idiosyncrasy for life! They can't be changed without years of therapy! And you think this little book is going to solve that?"

Be patient. More is coming.

Some psychologists say that in the first six years of life, we are functioning entirely in our subconscious brains. That means we have no ability to analyze what's going on around us with awareness.

As a result, most things we hear and experience from all the other people in our environment lands in our little subconscious minds.

Our computer minds absorb it all without reflection or discernment.

And that's when crud happens.

Distorted thinking occurs when what we experience includes something as innocent as not being held when we wanted to be held by mom. Or we heard our parents fighting and didn't understand why. We form judgments and beliefs about ourselves instead of viewing the scenes as possibly something else all together.

It could be that getting that special birthday gift was taken away and handed to a younger sister who chewed it. That could have greatly impacted me if I had decided as a kid, that others had the power to take things away from me at any time. I may have lived a life with that scenario and didn't understand why people were taking advantage of me.

Maybe it's a survival reflex from not being allowed to have a new coat for school, but a hand-me-down from a relative. Mom says, "We don't have money for new. Besides, you'll grow out of it soon enough."

Or how about, "Sorry son, we can't afford to send you to college. You'll have to work and wait if you still want to go."

Or, "Sorry daughter, we can't afford to send you to university. Besides, it's kind of a waste of time and money since you'll get married and raise kids anyway."

Or "Forget it! You're too stupid!"

Yes, that happens too!

We each installed millions of these impressions in our brains and called them Truth. I call them *Other Peoples Stuff!*

And let's remember that over 90% are *Other People's Stuff!* Less than 10 % of unconscious beliefs are yours. (Day 2)

Since we had no tools to decide what was right or wrong, we just left the impressions there, whether they were meant for us or not and whether they were rational or not. Then, as we grew older and acquired the skills of critical thinking, we never bothered to go back and revisit all those old impressions.

So guess what? They're still there. They are not your beliefs.

The good news is that you become aware of them.

ACTION STEP

Take out your pen and write the next steps. Here's a little secret. We've all been there. You are not alone.

Write down what your parents or other people in your life actually said and did that formed the belief you've just dug up from your childhood.

You're not worthy? You're not special? You feel ashamed? You feel sad? You feel less than?

Take your time because this step is very important to eliminate this belief. Write the one with the biggest emotional charge.

THE SOURCE of the belief is triggered by you interpreting their reactions when you didn't do what they wanted. You probably wanted to do something else.

Would you also say that many children who experienced what you did would come to the same conclusion as you did? Not really. Siblings in the same household tend to take on different beliefs and approaches to life over similar circumstances. Your story is your own.

You see, just acknowledging that it's other people's

judgments about your value, your worth, or anything else, literally reduces its power over you.

Giving your power away to others is equivalent to splitting yourself up into many versions of you. That means you are not whole and grounded and powerful to stay focused on what is true and valuable and worthy for you in the moment. Every time you are feeling overwhelmed, you are scattered and not all there. Let's correct that now. Let's pull your power back. How?

Bubbles! Yes, bubbles!

ACTION STEP

Set an egg timer for five minutes.

Use the page at the end of this chapter to write down your to-do list for today, tomorrow, next week and for the next six months! The list will include regular cleaning, laundry, shopping, special projects, writing, travelling, phone calls, social media time, stuff with your family, friends, and bath and bathroom breaks!

Now set the list aside and find a quiet place to sit. Close your eyes and take a deep breath.

What does this exercise have to do with your worthiness? Just this. Your list shows you what you choose to do alone, or with someone else, and other clues how you present yourself. If the list shows you hiding out, then you've just discovered a major belief.

Does this list make you feel worthy? Does asking for help make you feel less worthy?

Sit quietly with this for a moment.

Now, ask yourself, where is there tension and anxiety located in your body after you wrote this list? Trust yourself.

Now imagine a large bubble in front of you. Inside is a very powerful magnet. Allow the magnet to draw the anxiety out of you. "Swoosh!"

Look again into your body and ask for the next point of tension. Where else are you experiencing anxiety? Pull that out into the bubble.

And again until you have filled the bubble with collections of you feeling overwhelmed and stressed.

Look at the bubble and say "Hello, I see you. Hello, I see you. Hello, I see you."

Now say, "I see you God (or essence, or which ever spiritual word feels best for you). Repeat 2 more times. I see you God. I see you God."

Now put a second bubble beside the first one with a powerful magnet in it. Draw your power out of the first bubble.

Look at the first bubble and say, "I now release you from this form." And pop it!

Take your power from the 2nd bubble and bring it into your body. Allow the feeling of renewal and wholeness swirl around inside and outside of you.

That's it. Remember that if you get that feeling that you have so much to do, and you think it all has to be done only by you to prove you are worthy, do this popping exercise.

All those things you wrote don't all have to be done by you. No way. And they don't have to be done now. You are now open to receiving help, a change in activity, and support is now drawn to you. You've just discovered what triggers you and how to release the energetic pulse. Congratulations.

Great job today!

Chapter Seventeen

DAY 17: MANAGING STRESS

You must understand that the central theme of succeeding and tossing out beliefs that don't serve you in achieving success is as simple as taking responsibility for what you heard, saw and thought was real.

Everything revolves around your taking responsibility for your experiences. It doesn't matter who else was involved. When it comes to taking responsibility for what you experience, you either do or you do not. There is no in-between.

The Lakota Indians of North America say that the hurt of one, is the hurt of all, and the honor of one is the honor of all.

But how to get to that balance?

Stress builds quickly when you try to do too much and forget about feeling happy.

You've tried coping mechanisms. You did activities that you enjoyed. You accomplished and finished projects. You communicated your feelings and desires.

You are open to love and closeness. And you practice flexibility.

The truth is sometimes the outer resources are just not long-lasting and you find yourself back into stress modes.

The two areas that can minimize the negative effects of stress are nutrition and physical fitness.

ACTION STEP

Your brain works better with regular, nourishing food, activity, and drinking lots of water. So walk over to your junk food cupboard right now and toss out at least one bag of chips! That's it! Now go to the water cooler and fill a tall glass of cool water. Great job!

We try to apply the concept of balance. However, it makes more sense to apply moderation. You must be totally honest with yourself here. If you are not doing everything you know to stay healthy, then maybe you're not that committed to total health. What's keeping you stuck?

Look inside, bubble it out and reclaim your power.

ANOTHER ACTION STEP

Stand up. Now get those buns moving! You may not think exercise is for you, but let me share this. When you move your body, even if it's up and down a set of stairs once a day—with gusto—you move energy and manufacture more of it.

Here's the secret the yogis know: combining physical

and spiritual exercise like the ones throughout this booklet, can do more for your health, mind, wealth, emotional state, appearance and power.

Our bodies weren't meant to sit and veg. Take a look at elder people who don't move. They ache, muscles atrophy, their minds slow, and they veg.

You don't want that legacy, now do you? Here's the thing. If you suffer from exhaustion, guess what the remedy is? Not sleep. It's exercise.

Your body needs movement. So go ahead, get off your but(t) and move! Walk to the corner store instead of driving. Go for a swim, to the gym, or pull out a mat and do some sit ups right now on your living room floor. Lethargy is a culprit of thinking wrong thoughts. Get them out by moving them out. Energy moves from the inside as well as the outside.

Put on some music. Dance, sing, move!

Great job today!

Chapter Eighteen
DAY 18: INTERPRETATIONS

As you explore what you learned about your belief in a situation, you must also consider that the pain of one is the pain of all and the joy of one is the joy of all. We feel the pain of others, and they feel ours.

If our parents said or did something to hurt us, not only do we feel the sting, but they do as well.

That common suffering creates a sense of shared intimacy. And that's why sometimes it's so difficult to separate what is truth and what is *Other People's Stuff*.

Children put their parents on a pedestal. They believe most of what they are told.

But I'm here to tell you that if it isn't working out for you, let it go. And don't feel that you must hold them right or righteous.

Here's what I want you to think about next.

Where does meaning come from?

Yes, you're right, from your mind.

When you give meaning to an event, it's a fabrication of your mind.

So let me ask you this.

If meaning comes from your mind, is there any meaning inherent in your parent's behavior? Or is there any meaning inherent in any other events for that matter?

Of course, the answer is NO!

But as a child, we don't always know how to interpret this.

About other people. What do they know for sure about how good you are from how you were treated as a child?

They don't!

So why give your power to others when they don't know anything in the first place. They don't know you and they don't know what you want or what's best for you.

ACTION STEP

Take your power back. Close your eyes and imagine a hug bubble in front of you. Decide what you want to have happen today. Set an intention.

For example, today you may want to reduce and even totally release any fear about asking for a raise, or calling a special friend for a date, or simply finishing a project that has haunted you for some time.

Toss that intention into the bubble and add that you want it completed by the end of the day, or week. Add that you want it with ease, grace, love and fun.

Imagine a powerful golden beam of light filling the bubble from above. Imagine a strong wide beam running from below the bubble into the center of the earth. This grounds your manifestation.

Now say to the intention, "This or something better!" and release the grounding cord.

Send it into the universe to get worked on!

Great job today!

Chapter Nineteen

DAY 19: HAVINGNESS MASTERY

So up to now, you have been clearing some energy that no longer serves you. And you have been imagining and asking for what you do want. Are you in a receiving mode?

This is important because even though people ask for things, stuff gets in the way of actually receiving.

ACTION STEP

Find a quiet spot, relax and close your eyes. We've been working with bubbles and now let's add another device. Imagine a viewing screen in front of you. It looks like a large TV or a movie screen.

Now put a transparent bubble in front of you with the intention you set in the last exercise. It could have been a commitment to reducing fear, or calling a special friend, or whatever you would like to have for yourself.

On the screen see yourself receiving this thing and

enjoying it. Next to you imagine a gauge with numbers 1 to 100. This is your "Having" gauge.

Ask yourself how much "havingness" you currently have for the thing you want. Turn that dial up. Watch what happens when you move the dial.

As you raise the dial on the gauge, refocus on the bubble. Make sure the gold is flowing from above and make sure the bubble is grounded from below.

If you notice discomfort, lessen the intensity, and then dial up again. Do this until you feel comfortable receiving.

ANOTHER ACTION STEP

Now that you experience gauges and dials, imagine a second gauge called "Effort." Check to see how much effort you are using to do this exercise. If the dial is high, from 1 to 100, then turn the amount of effort down a notch. Notice how it feels. Now turn it back up. It can be that easy and that effortless.

Great job today!

Chapter Twenty

DAY 20: RECEIVING MASTERY

You have a desire. You sent it out to manifest. You reduced the amount of effort it takes and increased the amount of receiving.

So let's try another.

ACTION STEP

From now on, decide you will commit to allowing yourself to receive at least four things this month without saying anything in response except "Thank you."

You will want to practice receiving with gratitude. By the way, gratitude is one of the most powerful energetic glues to attract what you want!

Things that you could receive are compliments, gifts, smiles, money, love, hug or a handshake. Maybe you'll receive surprises! Welcome them and say, "Thank you."

In addition, give of yourself. Do something nice for someone else at least once a day. Giving is powerful manifestation energy because it shows the universe you are setting an example of what you want for yourself. Your gifts to others will be reciprocated. Generously accept what comes back to you.

Here's that powerful concept you will want to apply in your life:

Treat yourself the way you want to be treated!

Giving to yourself is mastering receiving for yourself. This is one of the most difficult concepts to initiate, yet one of the most powerful spiritual activities you can ever do.

To visualize receiving, find a nice quiet spot, close your eyes and take a deep breath.

Now imagine a golden river flowing towards you. You are standing ankle-deep in the river. Imagine the river swelling and flowing people, objects, money, love and joy towards you.

Open your arms and welcome the river of abundance. Allow yourself to receive whatever comes to you, embrace it, and enfold your treasures into your heart. That's it. Allow.

Chapter Twenty-One

DAY 21: MASTERING PEACEFULNESS

$\mathcal{A}$hh, to feel at peace and content with whatever is occurring around you. Ahhhh.

Events in themselves have no meaning and events with no meaning can't make you feel bad. So why is it that we allow an event to push our hurt and pain buttons?

Here's an example that could really set this notion in place for you, the notion of mastering peacefulness.

I look outside and I see clouds in the sky. In fact, clouds covered the day and night skies for the past week.

How do the clouds cause me to feel? Nothing. Nada. Don't care.

Now, an extraordinary event occurred recently. I experienced a total lunar eclipse, an event that happens once every 450 years when the sun, earth and moon are all directly aligned. You know it's happening because the moon turns a bright orange to blood read to dark brown caused by the deflection of sun's rays through our atmosphere.

The night of the eclipse, the clouds disappeared and I watched the eclipse excitedly and with joy. The question remains; what did the clouds cause me to feel? In this case, still nothing because they weren't a contention. If anything, I would probably feel good about clouds because they stayed away.

Now if the clouds had moved in, preventing a visual of the eclipse, how would the clouds then make me feel? I'd probably feel disappointed.

But is it really the clouds that made me feel bad? Or is it the meaning I'm giving the clouds.

Clouds have no meaning either way, good or bad. But give them one meaning and I feel good and then give them another meaning and I feel bad. This comes from my mind.

So the story you tell yourself, you know the one that leaves you feeling bad a lot of the time, is like the clouds. They have no meaning until you give them one.

See what I mean?

How do you know if the belief is completely gone? Say it out loud. You'll know if you have the belief if there is still an emotional resonance.

If you still have some resonance around the belief, you may want to bubble it out!

ACTION STEP

Imagine a bubble out in front of you. Inside the bubble is a powerful magnet. It can draw out any residual lingering of a belief. Just like metal filings are drawn to a magnet, the energy of that belief gets pulled into the bubble.

Now imagine a second bubble beside the first. It too has a powerful magnet. Point the magnet to the first bubble and pull out your power. Notice how the energy in the first bubble depletes and weakens.

Now pop the first bubble and allow it to disappear forever. You may say as you pop it, "I release you from this form."

Bring back your energy and power from that second bubble. Invite it back into you.

How can you tell if the belief is completely gone? Say it out loud and check in your gut how it resonates. Strong or dull. That's how you'll know.

People spend years eliminating beliefs. You just did it in moments.

Our mastery of feeling at peace with our experiences has to do with how we choose to view things.

From now on, make a commitment to give and receive positive energy!

Take a personal situation that triggers discomfort for you. How else can you interpret the event? That's the simplicity of mastering peacefulness: reframing and interpreting events differently.

Great job today!

Chapter Twenty-Two

CREATING SPACE IN A CROWD

Whether you live alone, with family, work by yourself or in a company of people, you will have connection and a strong support system to keep you grounded.

You've had people around you all your life. Now you know that if they give you advice that is contrary to your well-being, you know how to clear that out.

But that still leaves you with the dilemma of how to work and communicate with people on a daily basis without feeling they are in your space and you in theirs.

You will have mentors and advisors. You will attract new friends and people who help you learn at school and work. You will have people building you up and cheering you on. You will have people occasionally who put you down. So what to do?

ACTION STEP

First, do not underestimate the power of these visualizations or the ability of others to sense a shift in you. Before you come into contact with anyone, imagine a translucent rose in front of you. Make it giant! My own is at least three feet wide and ten feet high. Sometimes, depending on where I am, I surround myself completely with roses.

For men, imagine a staff with similar power.

The rose and staff have the energetic ability to absorb other people's energy before it gets into your space. Similarly, the rose and staff prevent your energy from getting into other people's space. The concept is you are taking charge of your own space and giving others permission to keep their own as well.

Try it. You will be pleasantly surprised at how people respond. They will notice something different, particularly those who enjoy being an in-your-face type of people. It's so cool and powerful at the same time.

Great job today!

Chapter Twenty-Three
TRANSFORM TO SELF-ESTEEM

You've now learned that it takes at least twenty-one days to form a new habit.

I aim to please, so I've given you more than twenty-one days of awe-inspiring, belief-busting and calm-generating tools to help you enjoy greater health, wealth, and other great things in life.

You now also know that we all form beliefs. That's life. But we can create the ones we want and let go of the ones we don't. Beliefs determine our life and now you know which of your beliefs will make your life work well and which you could let go!

Action Step

Life will overdeliver when you are in a receiving mode. Life will overdeliver when you are happy.

So, here's one more powerful exercise to help you continue your journey of discovery with ease.

THE MOST POWERFUL PERSON ON EARTH !

How to increase self-esteem to attract personal and professional relationships:

- Find a quiet spot, sit still, breathe and close your eyes.
- Get into the present moment by bringing all your energy and attention to the centre of your head.
- Connect with the center of the earth by imagining a cord from the base of your spine flowing down. Drop any energy which is not serving down that cord.
- Allow a gold beam of light to flood you from above, filling you inside and outside.
- Imagine a screen in front of you which is more like a mirror reflecting you back.
- Ask the mirror to show you the part of you which is strong. Notice what color that strength appears.
- Now ask to show you the part of you which is weak.
- If you see that part you don't like, ask to see the color of the energy behind the part that is weak. Wait to see the color. Patiently watch to see if anything changes. If you don't see a color, choose one yourself to distinguish this part from your strong part.
- Watch what happens.
- If there are no changes, imagine taking your whole image and releasing it into a bubble in

front of you. A powerful magnet inside that bubble pulls the image out of your screen.
- Now imagine a second bubble with another powerful magnet inside and pull your power out of the first bubble. Pop the first bubble and pull the second one into yourself.
- Now wipe the mirror clean with a golden sponge.
- Keep the gold light flowing down into you and keep the cord connecting you to the center of the earth solid and tight.
- Now see yourself in the mirror exactly as you would like to see yourself. Get creative with what you want physically and emotionally. Fit, lean body with a huge grin.
- Send appreciation to the image and bask in it until you feel complete acknowledging your self-esteem.

Great job today!

Remember, if you see any part inside you that does not please you, pull it out into a bubble, take your power back and resume appreciating yourself as you want to be.

After all who's the most powerful person on earth?

You Are!

BIBLIOGRAPHY

Bringhurst, Robert. *The Elements of Typographic Style*. Version 3.2. Point Roberts: Hartley & Marks, 2004.

Byrne, Rhonda, Law of Attraction: *The Secret*, NY Atria Books, 2006

Dyer, Wayne. *You'll See It When You Believe It: The Way to Your Personal Transformation.* NY: Harper Paperback, 2001

Gawain, Shakti, *Living in the Light: A Guide to Personal and Planetary Transformation.* Novoto, CA: New World Library, 1998

Hendricks, Gay, The Big Leap: Conquer Your Hidden Fear and Take Life to the Next Level, NY, Harper Collins, 2009

Hicks, Ester, Jerry Hicks, Abraham. *Ask and it is Given: Learning to Manifest Your Desires.* Carlsbad, CA: Hay House, 2004

Katz, Debra Lynne, *Freeing the Genie Within*, Llewellyn, 2009

LeBlanc, Mark, *Growing your Business! What You need to know what you need to do*, 2003

Morelli, David, Bubble Process, www.everythingisenergy.com 2009

Scheinfeld, Robert, *Busting Loose from the Business Game,* Wiley & Sons, 2009

Tamura, Michael J. *You Are the Answer: Discovering & Fulfilling Your Soul's Purpose.* Llewellyn, 2007

BIBLIOGRAPHY

The Chicago Manual of Style. 17th ed. The University of Chicago Press Editorial Staff. Chicago: The University of Chicago Press, 2017. https://www.chicagomanualofstyle.org/.

Zukav, Gary, *Spiritual Partnership, The Journey to Authentic Power,* 2010

ABOUT THE AUTHOR

For more than a decade, Patricia Ogilvie, a Certified Life and Energy Transformation Coach, has helped hundreds of small business owners transform their ideas, services, and products into viable online businesses. What she found was there are a lot of people, maybe you're one of them, who put added pressure and stress onto themselves when building deeper and relevant business relationships. That's what business is all about—building relationships. But why does it have to be stressful?

What Patricia does is help you dig deeper and help you take your own power back! She then guides you from the inside out by teaching unique, simple tools to unlock your fears, and frustrations and release your subconscious limiting beliefs that could be getting in the way of your business success.

You feel better, you have a mission, and you could even get to work on writing and publishing your book or e-book. This alone supports your business marketing with a pure, clear vision and intention. For personal and business success strategies, tools, editing, and formatting content to become recognized in your field of expertise, contact Patricia Ogilvie at Prorisk Enterprises Ltd.

www.ingramcontent.com/pod-product-compliance
Lightning Source LLC
Chambersburg PA
CBHW061335040426
42444CB00011B/2927